DREAM CATCHERS
CROCHET

A Creative Journey into the Art of Dreamcatcher Design

Contents

Introduction

"Dream Catchers Crochet" is a delightful and creative crochet book that offers a unique twist on the traditional art of crocheting. Written by a talented crochet artist, this book is a wonderful resource for both beginners and experienced crocheters alike who are looking to embark on a journey of crafting beautiful and intricate dream catchers using the versatile and soothing art of crochet.

Inside "Dream Catchers Crochet," you will find a collection of step-by-step crochet patterns and detailed instructions that will guide you through the process of creating stunning dream catchers. These dream catchers are not only aesthetically pleasing but also hold the symbolic power of capturing dreams and filtering out negativity, making them perfect for both decorative and spiritual purposes.

Whether you're looking to add a touch of boho chic to your home decor or simply want to explore a new and fascinating crochet project, "Dream Catchers Crochet" is your go-to resource. With its clear and easy-to-follow instructions, beautiful photography, and a variety of design options, this book is sure to inspire your creativity and help you bring your dream catchers to life through the art of crochet.

Crochet Basics

Materials and Equipments

1. Yarn

Whether or not you consider it a crochet tool, yarn might be the most fun material on the list. Big box and chain stores will probably have the largest, most affordable selection and offer yarns you can buy all year 'round. For more specialized products and services, check out local yarn shops staffed by knowledgeable crafters.

Factors on the yarn label that can influence your project include:

Thickness (fine, medium, bulky, etc.)
Fiber content (what the yarn's made of)
Weight in ounces or grams
Length in yards or meters
Tool suggestions (hook size)
Care instructions
In choosing yarn colors, pay attention to the lot number as well as the name of the color. Because yarn is dyed in batches, subtle differences exist, even within the same color from the same brand. The lot number ensures you're getting yarn from a specific batch.

2. Hooks

Every crochet hook has a handle (where you hold on), shank (between the handle and hook head and determines the hook size) and hook head (the part that grabs the yarn). After that, the variations are endless.

The most important variation is crochet hook size, designated by letters, numbers and millimeters. The millimeters provide the universal shank diameter, and the corresponding numbers and letters reflect a measurement system unique to the United States. While you're learning, try to use hook sizes recommended on your yarn labels.

Next select the kind of hook head you need:

- Inline hook heads are in line with the hook handle and have a deep groove (throat) to give you the most control over your yarn.
- Tapered hook heads protrude beyond the hook handle and have a shallow, more rounded throat.
- Hybrid hook heads are a middle ground between inline and tapered hook heads, and considered useful for the largest range of abilities and projects.

Choosing what your hooks are made of hinges on they type of yarn you'll use:

- Metal hooks are either shiny (for grippy, acrylic yarns) or matte (for smoother animal fiber yarns).
- Plastic hooks are affordable but don't work well with acrylic yarns, as the friction between the plastics creates a lag that takes a toll on the hands.
- Wooden hooks are inexpensive, high quality and work well with a range of yarn types.

Consider the ergonomics of your hooks, including handle thickness and curve and cushioning added around the hook itself. This will likely take some trial and error to see what feels best on your hands and wrists.

3. SCISSORS

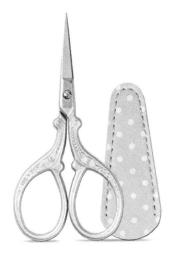

While any old scissors will work to snip your yarn, seasoned crocheters tend to prefer embroidery scissors. These small tools fit well in kits and often come in fun colors and designs.

You might also consider folding scissors as a safety and space-saving measure.

4. Tape Measure or Ruler

Keep a tape measure on hand for checking your gauge and measuring your crochet.

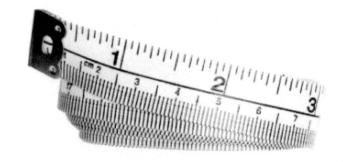

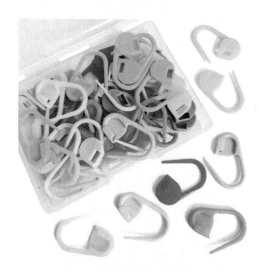

5. Stitch Markers

These can be hooked onto the crochet to mark a specific row or a specific stitch in the row, or to mark the right side of your crochet.

6. Pin cushion

A useful item to have by your side when working.

7. Row counter

These are useful for keeping track of where you are in your crochet. String on a length of cotton yarn and hang it around your neck— change it each time you complete a row.

6

Stitches and Techniques

Single Crochet (sc)

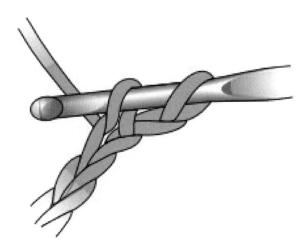

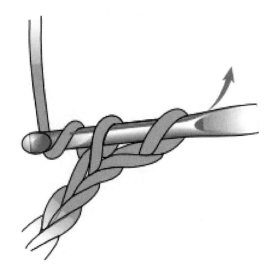

1. Insert the hook into the work (second chain from hook on the starting chain), *yarn over and pull up a loop.

2. Yarn over again and pull the yarn through both loops on the hook.

3. 1 sc made. Insert hook into next stitch; repeat from * in step 1.

7

Half Double Crochet (hdc)

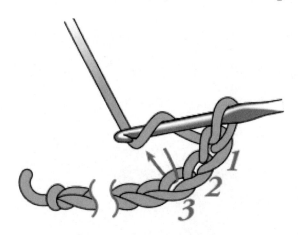

1. *Yarn over and insert the hook into the work (third chain from hook on the starting chain).*

2. ** Yarn over and draw through pulling up a loop.*

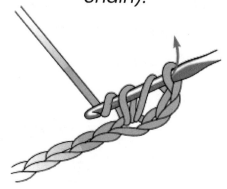

3. *Yarn over again and pull yarn through all three loops on the hook.*

4. *1 hdc made. Yarn over, insert hook into next stitch; repeat from * in step 2.*

Double Crochet (dc)

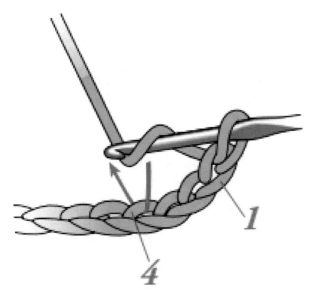

1. Yarn over and insert the hook into the work (fourth hain from hook on starting chain).

2. * Yarn over and draw yarn through pulling up a loop.

3. Yarn over and pull yarn through the first two loops only on the hook.

4. Yarn over and pull yarn through the last two loops on the hook.

5. 1 dc made. Yarn over, insert hook into next stitch; repeat from * in Step 2.

Treble (tr)

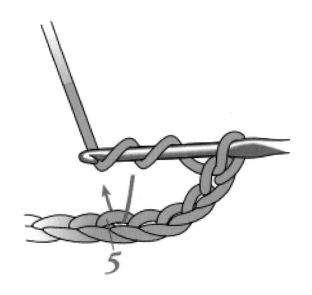

2. * Yarn over and draw yarn through pulling up a loop.

1. Yarn over twice, insert the hook into the work (fifth chain from hook on the starting chain).

3. Yarn over again and pull yarn through the first two loops only on the hook.

4. Yarn over again and pull yarn through the next two loops only on the hook.

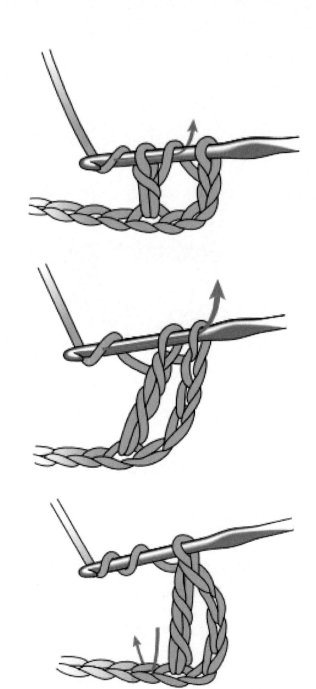

5. Yarn over again and pull yarn through the last two loops on the hook.

6. 1 tr made. Yarn over twice, insert hook into next stitch; repeat from * in Step 2.

Special Stitches

- **Standing Single Crochet:** Starting with a slip stitch on your hook, insert hook in stitch or space indicated and draw up a loop (two loops on hook). Yarn over and pull through both loops on your hook.
- **Standing Double Crochet:** Starting with a slip stitch on your hook, yarn over, insert hook in stitch or space indicated, yarn over and draw up a loop (three loops on hook). Yarn over and pull through two loops (two loops on hook). Yarn over and pull through both loops on your hook.
- **Cluster 2 (cl2):** Starting with a loop on your hook, *yarn over, insert hook in stitch or space indicated, yarn over and draw up a loop (3 loops on hook), yarn over and pull through two loops*, repeat from * once, yarn over and pull through all (4) loops.
- **Cluster 3 (cl3):** Starting with a loop on your hook, *yarn over, insert hook in stitch or space indicated, yarn over and draw up a loop (3 loops on hook), yarn over and pull through two loops*, repeat from * two times, yarn over and pull through all loops.

Abbreviations

- **St(s)** – stitch(es)
- **YO** – yarn over
- **Sk** – skip
- **Ch** – chain
- **Sp** – space
- **Sl st** – slip stitch
- **Sc** – single crochet
- **Hdc** – half double crochet
- **Dc** – double crochet
- **Tc** – triple crochet
- **Ps** – puff stitch
- **Picot** – tutorial provided below!
- **[]** – Repeat the instructions inside these brackets.
- **2DC Shell** - 2 DC sts into 1 st.
- **V Stitch** - DC, Ch1, DC in 1 st.
- **Picot** - Ch3, Sl St into first Ch
- **M1tb** - Make 1 top bar
- **Tss** - Tunisian Simple Stitch
- **lp/s** - loop/s
- **2dcl**-two double crochet cluster (explained below)

Dream Catchers Crochet

Crochet Dreamy Dreamcatcher

16

Materials

- Size 9 (1.4 mm) hook (a set like this would be perfect for a beginner)
- Cotton crochet thread, size 10 (I used Red Heart Classic Crochet Thread in Natural)
- Tapestry needle
- 7-inch metal ring (I got this set)
- jute cord or other material to wrap around metal ring
- lace, ribbons, flowers, feathers or whatever you prefer to decorate
-

Dimensions:

Approximately 5 inches in diameter unstretched

Instructions

ch 8, join to 1st ch with sl st

1) ch 3, (counts as dc, ch 1) [dc, ch1] 11 times, join to 2nd ch with sl st(total 12 dc, 12 ch-1 spaces)

2) sl st into ch 1 sp, ch 2, dc in same sp (counts as one 2dcl), ch 2, [in the next ch 1 sp, 2dcl, ch 2] repeat [] around, join to 2nd ch with sl st (total 12 clusters)

3) sl st into ch 2 sp, ch 6 (counts as dc, ch 4), [dc in next ch 2 sp, ch 4] repeat [] around, join to 2nd ch with sl st (total 12 dc, 12 "ch 4")

4) sl st into ch 4 sp, ch 10 (counts as tr, ch 7) [tr in next dc from previous row, ch 7] repeat [] around, join to 3rd ch with sl st (total 12 tr, 12 "ch 7")

5) sl st into ch 7 sp, ch 2, dc into ch 7 sp, ch 2 (counts as one 2dcl) [working in same ch 7 sp--{2dcl, ch 2} 2 times 2dcl], [in next ch 7 sp-2dcl {ch 2, 2dcl} 3 times] **4 total clusters in each ch 7 sp** repeat [] around, join to 2nd ch with sl st (total 48 clusters, 36 "ch 2")

6) ch 12 (counts as tr, ch 9), [tr in sp between the 2 2dcl without a "ch 2" in between them, ch 9], repeat [] around, join to 3rd ch with sl st (total 12 tr, 12 "ch 9")

7) sl st into ch 9 sp, ch 6, sk 4 ch, sc (in 5th ch), ch 3, sc in 5th ch again, ch 5, sc in tr, [ch 5, sk 4 ch, sc in 5th ch, ch 3, sc in 5th ch again, ch 5, sc in tr] repeat [] around

8) ch 16 (counts as sc, ch 15), [sc in sc from previous row that was worked into the tr st, ch 15] repeat [] around, join to 1st ch with sl st {total 12 sc, 12 "ch 15")

9) ch 6 (counts as sc, ch 5) [{ch 5, sk 3 ch, sc in next st} 3 times, ch 5, sk 3 ch, sc in sc from previous row] repeat [] around, join to 1st ch with sl st (total 48 sc, 48 "ch 5")

Fasten off, weave in ends.

To finish, I "blocked" my piece by ironing it flat.

Cheerful
Dreamcatcher

Materials:

- 1 ball Mille Colori Socks & Lace Luxe colour 53
- 1 ball Yarn and Colors Must-Have Minis colour 34
- Metal ring Ø 45cm
- Crochet hook 4mm
- Leftovers of ribbon or scraps of yarn in different colours

Tip:

- To make sure your dreamcatcher remains round you need to increase stitches in a different place each round. Increase 6 popcorn stitches each round.
- When your work tends to get lumpy then stop the increases and work one round without increasing. Then in the next round start increasing again. When your work still is lumpy then work another round without increasing.

Instructions

Start with a magic ring.

Round 1: Ch. 2, popcorn 1, ch. 3, repeat from *to* 5x. Close with sl.st. 1 in the first st. (6 popcorns)

Round 2: Sl.st. 1 in the 3-ch. space, ch. 2 *popcorn 1, ch. 3, popcorn 1, ch. 3 in the same ch. space, go to the next ch. space.* Repeat from *to* 5x. Close with a sl.st. 1 in the first st. (12 popcorns)

Round 3: Sl.st. 1 in the 3-ch. space, ch. 2, *Popcorn 1, ch. 3, go to the next ch. space, popcorn 1, ch. 3. popcorn 1, ch. 3 in the same ch. space, go to the next ch. space* Repeat from *to* 5x. Close with sl.st. 1 in the first st. (18 popcorns)

Round 4: Sl.st. 1 in the 3-ch. space, ch. 2 **Popcorn 1, ch. 3, popcorn 1, ch. 3 in the same ch. space, go to the next ch. space , popcorn 1, ch. 3, go to the next ch. space popcorn 1, ch. 3, go to the next ch. space* Repeat from *to* 5x. Close with sl.st. 1 in the first st. (24 popcorns)

Round 5: Sl.st. 1 in the 3-ch. space, ch. 2 *Popcorn 1, ch. 3, popcorn 1, ch. 3 in the same ch. space, go to the next ch. space, popcorn 1, ch. 3, go to the next ch. space, popcorn 1, ch. 3, go to the next ch. space, popcorn 1, ch. 3, go to the next ch. space* Repeat from *to* 5x. Close with sl.st. 1 in the first st. (6 times increasing = 30 popcorns)

Continue this way. Increase in the rows as is described below. Divide the increases such that your work remains nicely round.

Round 6: (36 popcorns) 6 increases

Round 7: (42 popcorns) 6 increases

Round 8: (48 popcorns) 6 increases

Round 9: (55 popcorns) 7 increases
Round 10: (61 popcorns) 6 increases
Round 11: (68 popcorns) 7 increases
Round 12: (68 popcorns) no increases
Round 13: (68 popcorns) no increases
Round 14: (68 popcorns) no increases
Round 15: (68 popcorns) no increases
Round 16: (75 popcorns) 7 increases
Round 17: (75 popcorns)

Finishing:

Work 17 rounds and join your dreamcatcher with sc. to the metal ring using Yarn and Colors Must-have Minis colour 34. Decorate your dreamcatcher with cheerful coloured ribbons or yarns.

Dreamcatcher Wall Hanging

Materials

- 15m of any 100% cotton DK yarn in white (we'd recommend the Sirdar Happy Cotton yarn)
- 3mm (UK10, US D/3) crochet hook
- 10cm (4") hoop
- Coloured felt
- Yarn needle, for sewing ends
- You will also need to print out this Feather template from issue 54

Measurements

- The finished crochet dreamcatcher is 10cm (4") diameter with a fringe approx. 12cm (4¾") long.

Instructions

Step 1

Ch8, ss to first ch to form a ring.

Step 2

Ch2 (counts as first dc in this round and all following), 15dc in ring, join into the top of the 2nd ch from start with a ss [16dc]

Step 3

Ch2, ch3, *miss 1 st, 1dc in next st, ch3; repeat from * to end of round finishing with miss 1 st, join into the top of the 2nd ch from start with a ss [8 3ch-sps]

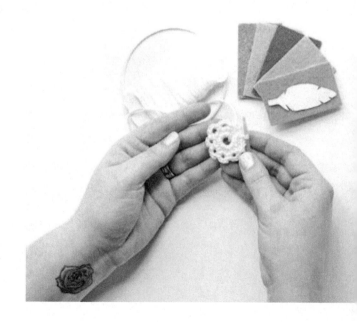

Step 4

Ss into first 3ch-sp, ch2, 3dc in same 3ch-sp, 4dc in each of next 7 3ch-sps, join into the top of the 2nd ch from start with a ss [32dc]

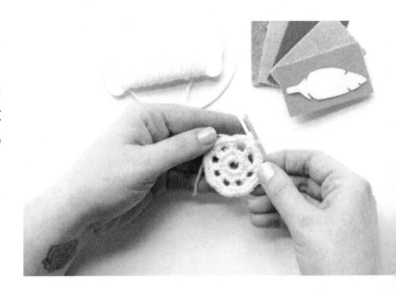

Step 5

Ch2, ch6, *miss 3 sts, 1dc in next st, ch6; repeat from * to end of round; finishing with miss 3 sts, join into the top of the 2nd ch from start with a ss [8 6ch-sps]

Step 6

Ss into first 6ch-sp, ch2, 3dc in same 6ch-sp, ch2, ss around hoop (note: here and at all ss on this round, hold yarn at back of hoop so when you do the next ch st you bring the yarn over the top of the hoop again, giving it an extra secure join), ch2, 4dc in the same 6ch-sp, ch2, ss around 10 cm hoop, ch2, *(4dc, ch2, ss around 10 cm hoop, ch2, 4dc, ch2, ss around 10 cm hoop, ch2) all in next 6ch-sp; repeat from * to end of round; join into the top of the 2nd ch from start with a ss. Break yarn, fasten off and sew in ends.

Finishing

Cut 12 x 25cm (9⅞") pieces of yarn and tie each one in half around the hoop to form the fringe. Using the feather template opposite, cut out five felt feathers and attach, with yarn, over the fringe. Make an 80cm (31½") chain as a tie and attach it to the top of the dreamcatcher for hanging.

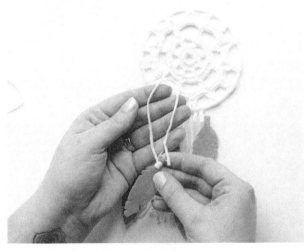

Tunisian Feathers Dreamcatcher

Finished Size:

-         Large Feather = 17 cm
-         Small Feather = 13 cm

Materials:

- 5mm crochet hook without handle (pop a rubber band on the end to keep your stitches from falling off)
- DK/8ply cotton in at least 2 colours

Instructions

Large Feather

Pattern notes:

- The following instructions are for the design pictured above (the little guy sitting out on his own) but you can go to town with as many colours as you like (or could be bothered weaving in the ends of), mix up the stripe sequence as you please. There are so many possibilities! Check out the photos throughout this post for inspiration.
- To clarify that the last stitch of the forward pass is worked differently, I always refer to this stitch in my patterns as an 'end stitch'
- Carry yarn between rows if there is only a few rows between colour changes. If there are more than a few rows, then it's best to cut yarn and rejoin.
- As you work, you will notice that your feather starts to lean to one side a little. That's a good thing! This will give your feather a nice natural shape

Foundation row: Using Colour A, ch 11. Starting from 2nd ch from hook, pick up a loop from the * top loop only of chain and in each ch to end (11 lps). Return

* a nicer edge is achieved for this design by working into the top loop instead of working from the usual back bump.

Row 2: M1tb, Tss 3, Tss3tog, Tss 3, M1tb, work end st (11 lps). Return

Row 3: Work as for Row 2, changing to Colour B on the last 2 lps of return

Row 4: Continuing with Colour B, work as for Row 2, changing to Colour A on the last 2 lps of return

Row 5: Continuing with Colour A, work as for Row 2, changing to Colour B on the last 2 lps of return

Row 6: Continuing with Colour B, work as for Row 2, changing to Colour A on the last 2 lps of return

Rows 7 – 10: Continuing with Colour A, work as for Row 2

Row 11: Work as for Row 2, changing to Colour B on the last 2 lps of return

Row 12: Continuing with Colour B, work as for Row 2, changing to Colour A on the last 2 lps of return

Row 13: Continuing with Colour A, Tss 3, Tss3tog, Tss 3, work end st (9 lps). Return changing to Colour B on the last 2 lps

Row 14: Continuing with Colour B, M1tb, Tss 2, Tss3tog, Tss 2, M1tb, work end st (9 lps), changing to Colour A on the last 2 lps of return

Rows 15 – 17: Continuing with Colour A, M1tb, Tss 2, Tss3tog, Tss 2, M1tb, work end st (9 lps). Return

Row 18: Tss 2, Tss3tog, Tss 2, work end st (7 lps). Return

Row 19: M1tb, Tss 1, Tss3tog, Tss 1, M1tb, work end st (7 lps). Return
Row 20: Tss 1, Tss3tog, Tss 1, work end st (5 lps). Return
Row 21: Tss3tog, work end st (3 lps). Return: − draw yarn through all 3 lps on hook. Ch 6, sl st back down along chain. Fasten off.
Weave in ends

Small Feather:

Pattern note: The following pattern doesn't include colour change instructions.
Foundation row: Ch 9. Starting from 2nd ch from hook, pick up a loop from the * top loop only of chain and in each ch to end (9 lps). Return
Rows 2 – 10: M1tb, Tss 2, Tss3tog, Tss 2, M1tb, work end st (9 lps). Return
Row 11: Tss 2, Tss3tog, Tss 2, work end st (7 lps). Return
Rows 12 – 13: M1tb, Tss 1, Tss3tog, Tss 1, M1tb, work end st (7 lps). Return
Row 14: Tss 1, Tss3tog, Tss 1, work end st (5 lps). Return
Row 15: Tss3tog, work end st (3 lps). Return: − draw yarn through all 3 lps on hook. Ch 6, sl st back down along chain. Fasten off.

Weave in ends
Tip: You can also make your feather in a single colour and embroider your designs on later

Loopy
Dreamcatcher

Materials:

- **Yarn:**

DMC Natura Just Cotton in the following colours. I crocheted each round in order of colour.

Col A – Amaranto

Col B – Spring Rose

Col C – Acanthe

Col D – Ble

Col E – Light Green

Col F – Jade

Col G – Aquamarine

Col H – Bleu Layette

Col I – Blue Jeans

- **Hook: Size** 3.5mm was used but I would recommend a 3.25mm to have the crocheted piece stretch more when attached onto the ring.
- Ring: 250mm ring (I used a Shamrock Craft Plastic Beige 250mm ring from Spotlight)
- Yarn needle
- Scissors
- Ribbon or lace of your choice

Instructions

Round 1:

Using Col A; in a magic ring, ch 3 (counts as dc), 15 dc in ring, jss to top of ch 3 made.
(16 dc)

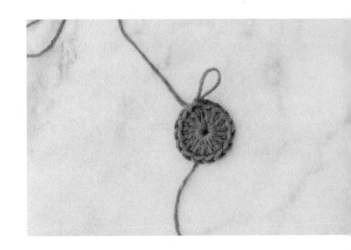

Round 2:

Using Col A; Ch 4 (counts as dc + ch), (dc + ch 1) in each st around, jss to 3rd ch made. Cut yarn and fasten off.
(16 dc, 16 x ch-1 sp)

Round 3:

Using Col B; In any ch-1 sp, make a standing cl2, ch 5, (cl2, ch 5) in each ch-1 sp around, jss to 1st cl2 made. Cut yarn and fasten off.
(16 cl2, 16 x ch-5 sp)

37

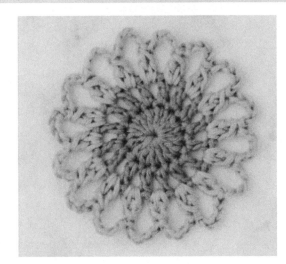

Round 4:

Using Col C; In any ch-5 sp, make a standing sc, ch 7, (sc, ch 7) in each ch-5 sp around, jss to 1st sc made. Cut yarn and fasten off.

(16 sc, 16 x ch-7 sp)

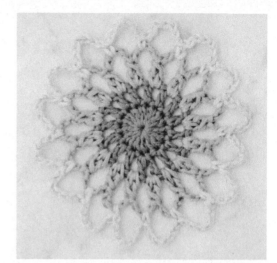

Round 5:

Using Col D; In any ch-7 sp, make a standing sc, ch 9, (sc, ch 9) in each ch-7 sp around, jss to 1st sc made. Cut yarn and fasten off.
(16 dc, 16 x ch-9 sp)

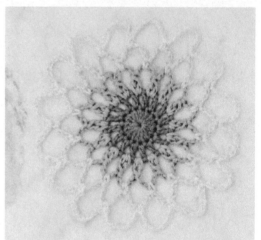

Round 6:

Using Col E; In any ch-9 sp, make a standing dc, 4 dc in same sp, ch 3, (5 dc, ch 3) in each ch-9 sp around, jss to 1st sc made. Cut yarn and fasten off.
(16 x 5 dc groups, 16 x ch-3 sp) **38**

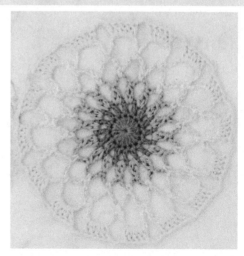

Round 7:

Using Col F; In any ch-3 sp, make a standing dc, (ch 3, dc) in same sp, ch 2, skip 2 dc, sc in next dc (middle dc of 5 dc group), ch 2, skip 2 dc, *v st in next ch-3 sp, ch 2, skip 2 dc, sc in next dc, ch 2, skip 2 dc*, repeat from * around, jss to 1st dc. Cut yarn and fasten off.
(16 x v st, 16 sc, 32 x ch-2 sp)

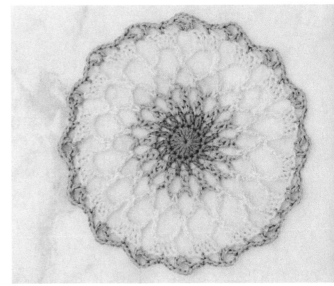

Round 8:

Using Col G; In any ch-3 sp from v st from round 7, make a standing cl3, ch 3, cl3 in same sp, ch 2, skip 2 ch sts, sc in sc from round 7, ch 2, skip 2 ch sts, *(cl3, ch 3, cl3) in next ch-3 sp, ch 2, skip 2 ch sts, sc in sc, ch 2, skip 2 ch sts*, repeat from * around, jss to top of 1st cl3 made. Cut yarn and fasten off.
(16 x [cl3, ch 3, cl3], 16 x sc, 32 x ch-2 sp)

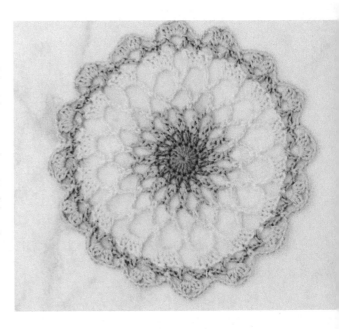

Round 9:

Using Col H; In any ch-3 sp made in round 8, make a standing dc, (ch 3, dc) in same sp, ch 1, skip 3 sts (cl3, 2 ch), v-tr in sc made in round 8, ch 1, skip 3 st (2 ch, cl3), *v st in ch-3 sp, ch 1, skip 3 sts, v-tr in sc, ch 1, skip 3 sts* repeat from * around, jss to 1st v st. Cut yarn and fasten off.
(16 x v st, 16 x v-tr, 16 x sc, 32 x ch-1 sp)

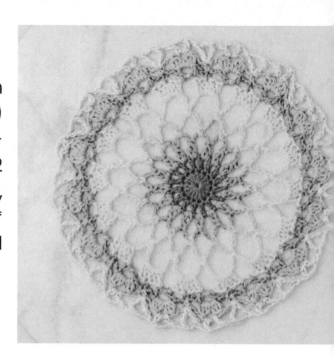

Round 10:

Using Col I; In any ch-3 sp (it doesn't matter if it's from the v st or v-tr st), make a standing *sc, (sc, ch 1 2 sc) in same sp, skip st, sc in ch-1 sp, skip st, (2 sc, ch 1, 2 sc) in ch-3 sp, skip st, sc in ch-1 sp, sk st*, repeat from * around, jss to 1st sc made. Cut yarn and weave in ends.
(160 sc, 32 x ch-1)

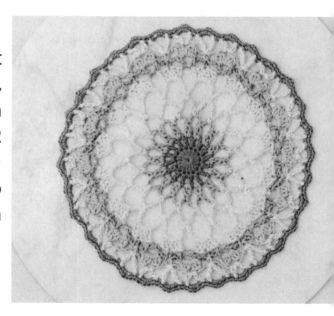

To attach to hoop, cut a piece of yarn the same material that you just used about 1m/40 inches. Thread onto needle, insert needle through ch-1 sp of any 'point' made in the last round, holding the crocheted part inside the hoop, thread needle under hoop, bringing it back over the top and into the next ch -1 sp, repeat around and fasten off, weave in yarn.

To get the same look as this new dream catcher, repeat this, but go the other way so you criss-cross over the ones already made.

Cut ribbon/lace into desired length and attach to bottom oh hoop using a slip knot method. I think it's called something like that, Fold ribbon in half and insert the middle (loop part) through the sp created when attaching crocheted part to hoop, pull wrap over the 'legs' of the ribbon, they just look like hanging legs to me lol, so that it creates a loop.

Daydreamer Dreamcatcher

Materials:

- Approximately 200 yards of any medium 4 worsted weight yarn
- Scrap Yarn
- Scrap Fabric
- 5.0 mm crochet hook
- Scissors
- Yarn Needle
- 4" Hoop (metal or embroidery hoop)
- 12" Embroidery Hoop
- Steamer (optional)
- **Yarn:**

A: 1 Skein of Yarn Bee Soft and Sleek Print Weight 4 Medium Worsted Yarn (100% acrylic, 186 yd/ 170 m, 4 oz/ 113 g) – Ivory Stripes (approx 80 yards used)

B: 1 Skein of Knit Pick's Brava Sport Weight 2 Yarn (100% premium acrylic, 273 yd/ 250 m, 3.5 oz/ 113 g) – White (approx 40 yards used)

Instructions

YO, and insert the hook in the st.

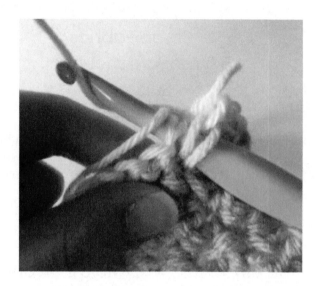

YO and draw up a loop – there should be 3 loops on the hook.

Rep Step 2, two more times – there should be 7 loops on the hook.

YO and pull through the first 6 loops on the hook – there should be 2 loops remaining on the hook.

YO and pull through the last 2 loops to close the st.

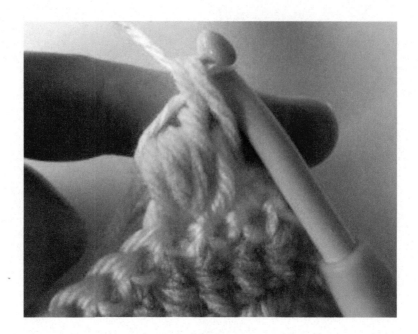

Mandala Dreamcatcher

Materials:

- Approximately 100 yards (or more) total of worsted weight (#4) cotton yarn. You can use up to 6 different colors. You can use any color combination you like or you can even make this in one solid color.
- I used 5 colors of (10-30 yards each). Hobbii Rainbow 8/8 100% Cotton yarn.
- Blue Color Fade color numbers: 70, 71, 32, 26, 1
- Purple Color Fade color numbers: 39, 68, 40, 67, 41, 1
- **Yarns**
  Threadart Cotton **
  Bernat Handicrafter Cotton**
  Lily's Sugar 'n Cream cotton yarn**
  Lion Brand 24/7 Cotton**
- **Notions**
  Crochet hook.5.5 mm (J). **
- Scissors **
- Yarn needle I used: Susan Bates Finishing Needles (Easiest to use) **
- Measuring tape **
- Craft Hoop 8-10" diameter**

Instructions

Note

I refer to Colors A, B, C, D, E, and F, however, you can use any color combination you like (for example 2 or 3 colors) including just one color.'

Pattern Chart is available in the PDF Version of this pattern.

For assistance with color changes, please refer to the video tutorial.

BEGIN:

[COLOR A] Chain 4 and join to first chain with a slip stitch to form a small circle.

Round 1: [COLOR A] Ch3 (counts as DC), 15 DC into circle. Join with sl st to first 3rd Ch. <<Stitch count: 16 DC>>

Round 2: [COLOR B] Ch4 (counts as DC, Ch1), (DC, Ch1) into each DC. Join with sl st to 3rd chain of first ch3.   <<Stitch count: 16 DC>>

Round 3: [COLOR C] In first ch1 space: (Ch3, DC, Ch1), (2DC shell, Ch1) in each ch1 sp of previous row. Join with sl st to 3rd chain of first ch3. Stitch count: 16 2DC shells and 16 Ch1 spaces.

Round 4: [COLOR D] In Ch1 space: (Ch4, DC, Ch1). (V Stitch, Ch1) in every ch1 space. Join with sl st to 3rd chain of first ch3. Stitch count: 16 V Stitches and 16 Ch1 spaces)

Round 5: [COLOR E] Join new color in ch1 of V stitch.

(Ch1, SC in same space as joined yarn, Ch2, Picot, Ch2). *(SC in next V stitch space, Ch2, Picot, Ch2) ** Repeat * to * to the end. Join with sl st to first SC.

Stitch count: 16 SC, 16 picots spaces

Round 6: [COLOR F]

Wrap yarn around crafting hoop tightly to cover entire hoop. Tie off with knot and cut a 30" tail.

Thread a yarn needle with the tail.

With the yarn needle go into the first picot of the mandala, pull yarn all the way through.

Then weave the yarn over the top of the hoop and back under.

Weave through next picot, over and under the hoop, and so on to the end.

Pull the tail tight fastening with a knot to the beginning.

Tie a loop of yarn for hanging.

Attach fringe to the bottom and voila! You're done!

Finishing

Sew in ends.

Doily Dreamcatcher

Materials:

- Embroidery Hoop (mine was 8 inches)
- Yarn (I used Red Heart Boutique Unforgettable Yarn, Dragonfly)
- Crochet Doily (8 inches or large enough to fit inside your hoop).
If you are a crocheter then by all means feel free to crochet your own doily!!
- Craft Feathers
- Pony Beads

Instruction

First wrap your yarn around the embroidery hoop. No need to glue. Just tie your yarn on and start wrapping!

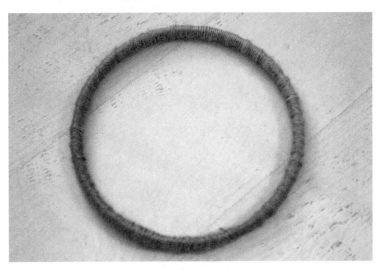

Cut 3 pieces of yarn and tie them to the bottom of your hoop. String on pony beads. Tie end of string onto feather.

Now you will want to attach the points of your doily onto the inside edges of the hoop. I found it easiest to use a tapestry needle to do this. You can even weave in the ends to make them as hidden as possible.

Create a loop of yarn on top so you can hang it on a bedroom wall or in front of the window.

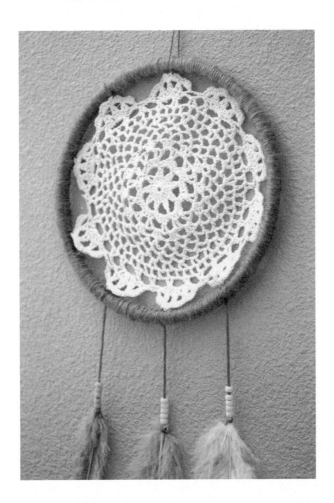

Vintage
Dreamcatcher

Materials

- DK cotton in 3 neutrals colors or just make your own choice using your favorites
- 2.5 mm crochet hook
- Ribbons in the same range of colors chosen. You can play with some different textures and widths
- Embroidery hoop. I recommend to get the hoop after crochet the main piece
- Tapestry needle
- Scissors

Instructions

Make a magic ring or ch 4 and join with a slip stitch in the first ch.

Row 1: ch 1 (does not count as stitch), make 16 sc into the ring. Join with a slip stitch in the first stitch.

Row 2: ch 2 (counts as stitch), skip 1 stitch, ch 3, * dc in the next stitch, skip 1 stitch, ch 3 **. Repeat from * to ** the entire row. Join with a slip stitch in the first stitch.

Row 3: ch 2 (counts as stitch), 1 dc in the next 2 stitches, ch 5, * dc in the next 3 stitches, ch 5**. Repeat from * to ** the entire row. Join with a slip stitch in the first stitch.

Row 4: ch 2 (counts as stitch), (yarn over, place hook in next stitch, yarn over, pull through stitch, yarn over, pull through 2 loops) twice. Yarn over, pull yarn through all loops for a completed decrease, ch 5, sc in the ch-5 space from previous row, *ch 5, dc decrease triple in the next 3 stitches, ch 5, sc in the next ch-5 space,**. Repeat from * to ** the entire row until get the last ch-5 space, ch 2, dc in the first decrease stitch (doing this, the yarn will stay in the center of the last ch space)

Fasten off and cut the yarn. Leave a long tail to attach to the hoop. Sew the first end.

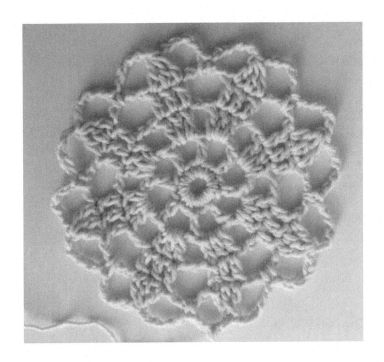

Small flower

ch 20, 4 dc in the third ch, skip 1 ch, * sc in the next ch, 5 dc in the next ch, **
Repeat from * to ** the entire chain. Fasten off and cut a long tail. Roll to make the flower and sewn it.

Medium flower

ch 24, sc in the second ch, * (hdc, 3 dc, hdc) in the next ch, sc in the next ch**
Repeat from * to ** the entire chain. Fasten off and cut a long tail. Roll to make the flower and sewn it.

Large flower

ch 38, sc in the second ch, *(hdc, 3 dc, hdc) in the next ch, sc in the next ch** Repeat from * to ** 4 times

*skip 1 ch, (hdc, 3 dc, hdc) in the next ch, skip 1 ch, sc in the next ch** Repeat from * to ** 4 times

*skip 1 ch, (hdc, 5 dc, hdc) in the next ch, skip 1 ch, sc in the next ch** Repeat from * to ** 3 times. Fasten off and cut a long tail. Roll to make the flower and sewn it.

Assemble

Using the long tail, attach the work to the inner hoop as is pictured below.

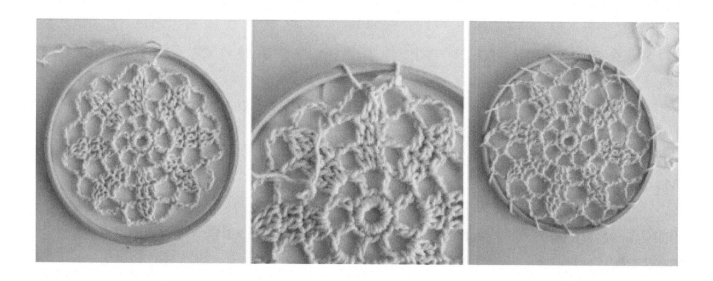

Cut the ribbons with a minimum of 60 cm, attach one at a time to the outer hoop until you get your desired look.

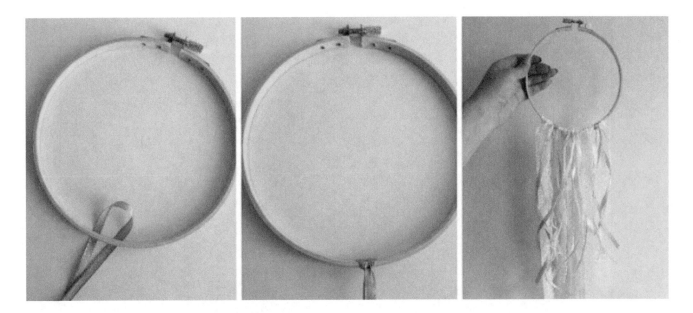

Attach the flower to one side of the ribbons from little one to large one. I used hot glue but this is optional, you can knot them to the hoop with its yarn tails.
Put the inner hoop in place and secure, use some ribbon to make a knot in the top and it's ready to hang.

Star Dreamcatcher

Materials

- 1 ball Aunt Lydia's Crochet Thread Fashion 3 (super fine weight) 150yd/137 m in White
- US 2 (2.2 mm) crochet hook
- size 6/0 glass beads - 46 beads each of three different colors
- collapsible eye beading needle
- 10 inch metal ring
- assortment of ribbon, yarn or string for embellishing

Gauge

24 sts and rows in sc = 4 inches

Instruction

Begin by stringing the beads onto your yarn in the following pattern: [ABC] 2 times, [AABBCC] 10 times, [ABC] 24 times.

Note: The last bead you string onto your yarn will be the first bead you crochet into the design.

The entire piece is worked in continuous rounds with the wrong side facing. The beads will be on the back of your work as you crochet.

Ch 5, sl st in first ch to form a loop.

Rnd 1: *Ch 4, sc in loop* 6 times.

Rnd 2: *Ch 4, 2 sc in next ch 4 space* 6 times.

Rnd 3: *Ch 4, 2 sc in next ch 4 space, sc in next sc* 6 times.

Rnd 4: *Ch 4, 2 sc in next ch 4 space, slb, sc in next 2 sc* 6 times.

Rnd 5: *Ch 4, 2 sc in next ch 4 space, sc in next sc, slb, sc in next 2 sc* 6 times.

Rnd 6: *Ch 4, 2 sc in next ch 4 space, sc in next 2 sc, slb, sc in next 2 sc* 6 times.

Rnd 7: *Ch 4, 2 sc in next ch 4 space, sc in next 3 sc, slb, sc in next 2 sc* 6 times.

Rnd 8: *Ch 4, 2 sc in next ch 4 space, sc in next 4 sc, slb, sc in next 2 sc* 6 times.

Rnd 9: *Ch 4, 2 sc in next ch 4 space, sc in next 5 sc, slb, sc in next 2 sc* 6 times.

Rnd 10: *Ch 4, 2 sc in next ch 4 space, sc in next 6 sc, slb, sc in next 2 sc* 6 times.

Rnd 11: *Ch 4, 2 sc in next ch 4 space, sc in next 7 sc, slb, sc in next 2 sc* 6 times.

Rnd 12: *Ch 4, 2 sc in next ch 4 space, sc in next 8 sc, slb, sc in next 2 sc* 6 times.

Rnd 13: *Ch 4, 2 sc in next ch 4 space, sc in next 9 sc, slb, sc in next 2 sc* 6 times.

Rnd 14: *Ch 4, 2 sc in next ch 4 space, sc in next 10 sc, slb, sc in next 2 sc* 6 times.

Rnd 15: *Ch 4, 2 sc in next ch 4 space, sc in next 11 sc, slb, sc in next 2 sc* 6 times.

Rnd 16: *Ch 4, sc in next ch 4 space, ch 4, skip 1 sc, sc in next sc, slb, sc in next 10 sc, slb, sc in next 2 sc* 6 times.

Rnd 17: *[Ch 4, sc in next ch 4 space] 2 times, ch 4, skip 1 sc, sc in next sc, slb, sc in next 8 sc, slb, sc in next 2 sc* 6 times.

Rnd 18: *[Ch 4, sc in next ch 4 space] 3 times, ch 4, skip 1 sc, sc in next sc, slb, sc in next 6 sc, slb, sc in next 2 sc* 6 times.

Rnd 19: *[Ch 4, sc in next ch 4 space] 4 times, ch 4, skip 1 sc, sc in next sc, slb, sc in next 4 sc, slb, sc in next 2 sc* 6 times.

Rnd 20: *[Ch 4, sc in next ch 4 space] 5 times, ch 4, skip 1 sc, sc in next sc, slb, sc in next 2 sc, slb, sc in next 2 sc* 6 times.

Rnd 21: *[Ch 4, sc in next ch 4 space] 6 times, ch 4, skip 1 sc, sc in next sc, slb, sc in next 2 sc* 6 times.

Colorful Dream Catcher

66

Size/Measurements:

14"x14"

Materials

- Yarn: Red Heart Croquette (1 cake)
- Color: Calming
- Hook: E (3.50 mm)
- Ribbons (optional)
- Silver Hoop – 14 inch (35.5 cm)
- Yarn needle
- **Yarn Label Information:**

  Red Heart Croquette
- Yarn Weight: Super Fine #1
- Cake: 239 yards / 219 meters
- Unit Weight: 45 grams (1.5 ounces)
- Fibers: 92% Cotton: 5% Polyester, 3% Other

Instruction

Notes:

1. Begin work from center of cake. Cut yarn, wind up in separate balls to get to the next color.
2. Work in the Round.
3. Ch 1 does not count as a stitch throughout, unless otherwise noted.
4. Stitch counts are in ( ) at the ends of the Rounds.
5. Right side is always facing, do NOT turn.

Ch 5 (counts as 1 tr and 1 ch).

Round 1: 1 tr in 5th ch from hook, *ch 2, 2 tr in same ch, repeat from * 6 more times, end with ch 2, sl st to top of beg ch-5. (16 tr, 8 ch-2 sps).

Round 2: sl st into ch-2 sp, ch 1, *3 sc in ch-2 sp, skip 2 tr, repeat from *, end with skip 2 tr, sl st to beg sc. (24 sc).

Round 3: [ch 6, sl st in next st] 23 x, end with ch 3, 1 dc in base of beg ch-6. (23 ch-6 sps, 1 ch-3/dc sp). Measures 3".

Round 4: ch 1, sc in same sp, *ch 3, sc in next ch-6 sp, repeat from *, end with ch 3, sl st to beg sc. (24 ch-3 sps).

Round 5: sl st into ch-3 sp, ch 1, *3 sc in ch-3 sp, skip 1 sc, repeat from *, end with skip 1 sc, sl st to beg sc. (72 sc). Measures 3.75".

Round 6: ch 1, sc in same st, [ch 3, skip 2 sts, 1 sc in next st] 23 x, end with ch 1, 1 dc in beg sc. (23 ch-3 sps, 1 ch-1/dc sp).

Round 7: ch 1, sc in same st, [ch 4, 1 sc in next ch-3 sp] 23 x, end with ch 2, 1 dc in beg sc. (23 ch-4 sps, 1 ch-2/dc sp).

Round 8: Repeat Round 7. (23 ch-4 sps, 1 ch-2/dc sp). Measures 5″, end off yarn.

Blue-Violet color: place slip knot on hook. Begin in any ch-4 space.

Round 9: 1 sdc, 2 dc in same sp, *fpdc around sc, 5 dc in next ch-4 sp, repeat from *, end with fpdc around sc, 2 dc in beg ch-4 sp, sl st to beg dc. (120 dc, 24 fpdc).

Round 10: ch 3, 1 dc in same st, ch 2, 2 dc in same st, *skip 2 sts, 1 fptr around fpdc, skip 2 sts, shell in next st, repeat from *, end with skip 2 sts, 1 fptr around fpdc, sl st to top of beg ch-3. (24 shells, 24 fptr).

Round 11: sl st into ch-2 sp, ch 3, 2 dc, ch 2, 3 dc, in same sp, *1 fptr around fptr, dbl shell in shell, repeat from *, end with 1 fptr around fptr, sl st to top of beg ch-3. (24 dbl shell, 24 fptr).

Round 12: Repeat Round 11. (24 dbl shell, 24 fptr). Measures 10″, end off yarn.

Mint green color: place slip knot on hook. Begin in any ch-2 sp.

Round 13: 1 ssc in ch-2 sp, *ch 6, sc in next ch-2 sp, repeat from *, end with ch 3, 1 tr in beg sc. (24 ch-6 sps).

Round 14: ch 1, sc in same sp, *ch 7, sc in next ch-6 sp, repeat from *, end with ch 4, 1 tr in beg sc. (24 ch-7 sps).

Round 15: Repeat Round 14. (24 ch-7 sps). Measures 11″.

Note: It needs to be approximately 2 inches smaller than the hoop when completed. This will allow for it to stretch inside the hoop. If it is too large, try hdc on the next round instead of dc, or you could omit the next round altogether and skip to Assembly. You would attach in the same way, just going through each ch-7 space instead.

Round 16: ch 4 (counts as 1 dc, ch1) 5 dc in same sp, *ch 1, [5dc, ch1, 5dc] in next ch-7 sp, repeat from *, end with ch 1, 4 dc in beg ch-7 sp, sl st to 3rd ch of beg ch 4. (240 dc, 48 ch-1 sps). Measures 12".

End off yarn, weave in ends.

Assembly:

Chain 350 with Mint green, remove hook, place 1 stitch marker in live loop.

Place work inside the 14" hoop. Attach stitch marker (with the live loop) to the hoop.

Using the chain tail, wrap around the hoop 1 time, pull through ch-1 sp, *wrap around hoop, pull through next ch-1 sp, repeat from *. Once all ch-1 sps are attached, the chain tail should be at the stitch marker.

Remove stitch marker, insert hook in live loop, make additional chains to the length of the chain tail to form the loop to hang it, end off yarn.

Tie both ends of the chain in a knot against the hoop 2 times to secure it, knot the ends together leaving space (3 to 4 inches) to hang it up.

Embellish: (optional) attach ribbons, beads, feathers, or other materials from the bottom of the hoop to hang down as a decorative element.

Fall Dreamcatcher

Materials:

- embroidery hoops of different sizes (2)
- hemp (or string)
- yarn
- beads (or charms)
- feathers
- acorns, branches, leaves , etc.
- scissors
- glue

72

Instruction

Start by making your yarn moon! Bind the two embroidery hoops together at one spot and as the hoop edges diverged, begin wrapping the yarn between the two in a "figure 8" pattern.

Create your hanging accents! Wrap a stick or branch with hemp at the top and tie off. No fancy knots here – just tie securely and be sure to leave enough tail to tie the piece to the bottom of the dream catcher. Feather tip: After you tie on the hemp, add a bead and if it will fit, push the bead over the top of the feather point.

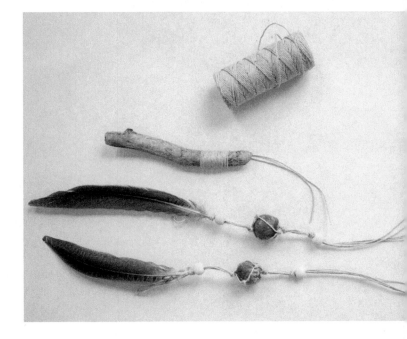

Here comes the most important part: weaving your dream catcher! Looks complicated but it's just the same knot made over and over again.

You always want to enter the hoop from back to front and then drop the end of the hemp through the loop you just created. Pull tight and then make your next knot! For the first round, evenly space the knots around the hoop and make sure your last knot is made right next to your first. Once you've made the round, begin making the knots on the hemp loops you just created from your last round. Continue until your heart is content! We left space in the middle in case we want to add a charm to hang in the middle of the opening.

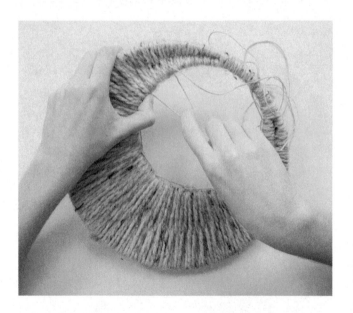 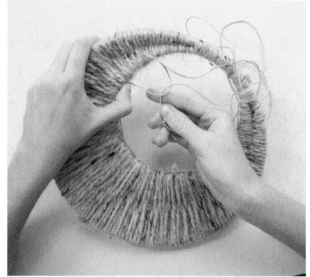

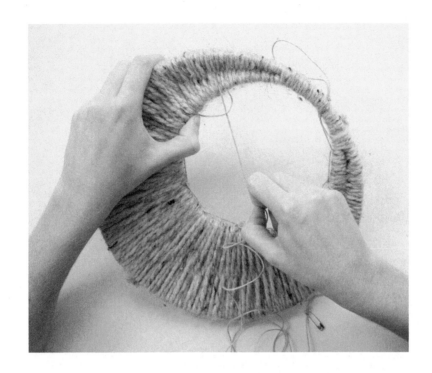

Once the base is made, tie on your hanging accents and add some greenery!

Printed in Great Britain
by Amazon

42072790R00044